pilgrim

THE BIBLE
A COURSE FOR THE CHRISTIAN JOURNEY

Church Publishing
NEW YORK

Authors and Contributors

Authors

Stephen Cottrell is the Bishop of Chelmsford
Steven Croft is the Bishop of Sheffield
Paula Gooder is a leading New Testament writer and lecturer
Robert Atwell is the Bishop of Exeter
Sharon Ely Pearson is a Christian educator in The Episcopal Church

Contributors

Vivienne Faull is Dean of York
Rosemary Lain-Priestley is Dean of Women and Chair of the Church of England's national network of advisers in women's ministry
David Moxon is the Archbishop of Canterbury's Representative to the Holy See and Director of the Anglican Center in Rome

pilgrim

pilgrim

THE BIBLE
A COURSE FOR THE CHRISTIAN JOURNEY

STEPHEN COTTRELL
STEVEN CROFT
PAULA GOODER
ROBERT ATWELL
SHARON ELY PEARSON

Contributions from
VIVIENNE FAULL
ROSEMARY LAIN-PRIESTLEY
DAVID MOXON

Church Publishing
NEW YORK

Cover image—Mimadeo/Shutterstock.com

ISBN-13: 978-0-89869-954-8 (pbk.)
ISBN-13: 978-0-89869-955-5 (ebook)

First published in the United Kingdom in 2014 by

Church House Publishing
Church House
Great Smith Street
London SW1P 3AZ

First published in the United States in 2016 by

Church Publishing, Incorporated.
19 East 34th Street
New York, New York 10016
www.churchpublishing.org

Cover and contents design by David McNeill, Revo Design.

Library of Congress Cataloging-in-Publication data

A record of this book is available from the Library of Congress.

Printed in the United States of America

CONTENTS

WELCOME TO *PILGRIM*

Welcome to this course of exploration into the truth of the Christian faith as it has been revealed in Jesus Christ and lived out in the Church down through the centuries.

The aim of this course is to help people explore what it means to be disciples of Jesus Christ. From the very beginning of his ministry, Jesus called people to follow him and become his disciples. The first disciples were called to be with Jesus and to be sent out (Mark 3:14). The Church in every generation shares in the task of helping others hear Christ's call to follow him and to live in his service.

The *Pilgrim* material consists of two groups of four short courses. The **Follow** stage is designed for those who are beginning to explore the faith and what following Jesus will mean. It focuses on four great texts that have been particularly significant to Christian people from the earliest days of the Church:

● The Baptismal Covenant (drawn from the Creeds)

● The Lord's Prayer

● The Beatitudes

● The Commandments

The Follow stage is a beginning in the Christian journey. There is much still to be learned. The four courses in the **Grow** stage—of which this is one—aim to take you further and deeper, building on the Follow stage. They focus on:

● The Creeds

● The Eucharist (and the whole life of prayer and worship)

- The Bible
- The Church and the kingdom (living your whole life as a disciple)

We hope that, in the Grow stage, people will learn the essentials for a life of discipleship. We hope that you will do this in the company of a small group of fellow travelers: people like you who want to find out more about the Christian faith and are considering its claims and challenges.

The material in the Grow stage can also be helpful to people who have been Christians for many years, as a way of deepening their discipleship.

We have designed the material in the Grow stage so that it can be led by the members of the group: you don't need an expert or a teacher to guide you through. *Pilgrim* aims to help you learn by encouraging you to practice the ancient disciplines of biblical reflection and prayer which have always been at the heart of the living out of Christian faith.

The format is similar to the Follow stage. Each book has six sessions and, in each session, you will find:

- a **theme**
- some **opening prayers**
- a **"conversation-starter"**
- an opportunity to reflect on a **reading** from Scripture (the Bible)
- a short **reflection** on the theme from a contemporary Christian writer
- some **questions** to address together
- a **"journeying on"** section
- some **closing prayers**
- finally, there are selected quotations from the great tradition of Christian writing to aid further reflection.

You will find a greater emphasis in the Grow stage on learning to tell the story of God's work in your life to others as every disciple is called to be a witness. You will also find a greater emphasis on learning to live out your faith in everyday life. The Journeying On section includes an individual challenge for the week ahead and you are encouraged to share your progress as part of the Conversation as you meet for the next session.

INTRODUCTION TO *THE BIBLE*

The Bible is one of the most influential books in the world. It is still far and away the bestselling book worldwide, and it is estimated that over six billion copies have been sold or given away. It has influenced films and plays, literature, art, and music. So great is its influence on the Western world that it can be difficult to understand some of these properly without a working knowledge of the Bible's contents. This is not, however, why Christians read the Bible. We read the Bible because by doing so, we believe that we will hear God speaking and learn more about who God is and what God has done for us.

The Bible contains the sacred Scriptures of both Judaism and Christianity. The first 39 books of the Bible comprise the Jewish Scriptures and are called by Christians the Old Testament—or Hebrew Scriptures. The final 27 books make up the New Testament and are sacred only to Christians. The Christian names for the collections refer to the belief that God created covenants or testaments with people throughout history. The Old Testament tells the story of the making and breaking of more than one covenant between God and people. The New Testament records what Christians consider to be the making of another and final covenant through the death and resurrection of Jesus, a covenant that is remembered in the sharing of bread and wine in Holy Communion. In many Bibles, especially those used by Roman Catholics and Episcopalians, there is a third section: fifteen books called the Apocrypha. These are additional books from the Hebrew people's sacred story.

The Catechism of The Episcopal Church reflects the importance the Church places on the Bible in six questions and answers (a Catechism is the authorized teaching of the Church for new Christians).

The first four questions and answers reflect this:

Q: What are the Holy Scriptures?

A: The Holy Scriptures, commonly called the Bible, are the books of the Old and New Testaments; other books, called the Apocrypha, are often included in the Bible.

Q: What is the Old Testament?

A: The Old Testament consists of books written by the people of the Old Covenant, under the inspiration of the Holy Spirit, to show God at work in nature and history.

Q: What is the New Testament?

A: The New Testament consists of books written by the people of the New Covenant, under the inspiration of the Holy Spirit, to set forth the life and teachings of Jesus and to proclaim the Good News of the Kingdom for all people.

Q: What is the Apocrypha?

A: The Apocrypha is a collection of additional books written by people of the Old Covenant, and used in the Christian Church.

The fifth question and answer looks at the connection of how we understand the origins of the Bible and why it is important to us today. There were (at least) two stages of how these writings came to be called Holy Scripture. The actual writing of these books came first, many handed down for generations orally before they were collected and written. Hundreds of years later the choosing of these over other books and writings formed what is known as the "Canon" (the authorized books of sacred writing that was formally set for Christians in the 7th century CE). The Bible, as we know it today, has a fixed form.

Q: Why do we call the Holy Scriptures the Word of God?

A: We call them the Word of God because God inspired their human authors and because God still speaks to us through the Bible.

Great importance is attributed to the Holy Spirit in all the stages of how the Bible came to be and how we read the Bible today. We read the Bible today because we believe that God will speak to us and in speaking to us reveal to us what we should do.

Q: How do we understand the meaning of the Bible?
A: We understand the meaning of the Bible by the help of the Holy Spirit, who guides the Church in the true interpretation of the Scriptures.

Reading the Bible is not an optional extra that we should do if we can find the time. It is an essential part of our Christian life and journey. Being a disciple of Jesus means to be someone who yearns to learn more and more about him. In reading the Bible we listen to how God speaks to us individually, and how the words of Scripture draw us into the conversation of the church about the work of Christians in the world. We learn of God's relationship with the world, as well as our personal way of living.

The six sessions of this course all explore the subject of these six questions in a little more detail. It cannot hope to explore them in full. It is highly likely that you will reach the end of the course with many questions unanswered. You may, in fact, reach the end of the course with even more questions than you began with, but the study of the Bible can be like that. The more you know, the more you realize you need to know.

The first session will pick up the first question—"What is the Bible?"—and reflect on the Bible and its contents. The second and third sessions ("The Bible as Breath" and "The Bible as a Stream of Living Water") both look in more detail at the inspiration of the Bible by the Holy Spirit and the importance of the whole Canon of Scripture for our faith. The fourth and fifth sessions ("The Bible as a Lamp" and "The Bible as a Two-Edged Sword") explore the question of how and why we read the Bible, and the sixth and final session will make some more practical suggestions about how you make reading the Bible a part of your daily life.

The titles for sessions 2-5—the Bible as breath, as water, as a lamp, and a two-edged sword—may appear to be a somewhat random collection of images. They are here because they are some of the ways the Bible talks about itself and as such are a very good way for us to begin thinking about the Bible and how we read it.

Psalm 1:1-3: Happy are those who(se)...delight is in the law of the LORD, and on his law they meditate day and night. They are like trees planted by streams of water.

Psalm 119:105: Your word is a lamp to my feet and a light to my path.

Hebrews 4:12: Indeed, the word of God is living and active, sharper than any two-edged sword.

2 Timothy 3:16: All scripture is inspired by God and is useful for teaching, for reproof, for correction, and for training in righteousness.

It is fascinating to notice that the Bible itself gives us hints and tips about how best to read it, as something:

- that is inspired or breathed out by God
- that gives us nourishment like water does to a tree
- that sheds light on our darkest path
- that with the accuracy of a sharpened sword separates things one from another.

At the end of these six sessions the Bible will not suddenly become much easier to read. It is a large collection of books, long and sometimes hard to understand. Not only that, but it was also written into a world very different from our 21st-century world. But at the end of these six sessions we hope that you will have caught a glimpse of the joy as well as the importance of persevering with your reading. We also hope that you will have learned a few more tips about how to make reading the Bible a part of your everyday life. To help in this, each week the "Journeying On" section of the course contains six verses from the Bible. We would encourage you to reflect on one of these each day between the sessions: read it, pray about it, listen to what God might be saying to you in it, and allow it to change you.

PAULA GOODER

The Lord's Prayer

Our Father in heaven,
hallowed be your name,
your kingdom come,
your will be done,
on earth as in heaven.
Give us today our daily bread.
Forgive us our sins
as we forgive those who sin against us.
Save us from the time of trial,
and deliver us from evil.
For the kingdom, the power,
and the glory are yours,
now and for ever. Amen.

CONTEMPORARY LANGUAGE VERSION

Our Father, who art in heaven,
hallowed be thy name;
thy kingdom come;
thy will be done;
on earth as it is in heaven.
Give us this day our daily bread.
And forgive us our trespasses,
as we forgive those who trespass against us.
And lead us not into temptation;
but deliver us from evil.
For thine is the kingdom,
the power, and the glory,
for ever and ever. Amen.

TRADITIONAL LANGUAGE VERSION

(For use in the Concluding Prayers of each session)

WHAT IS THE BIBLE?

pilgrim

In this session we are looking at a "way in" to reading the Bible, thinking particularly about how to recognize what kind of writing you are reading.

Opening Prayers

Comfort, O comfort my people, says your God.
The word of the Lord endures for ever.
All flesh is like grass and all its glory is like the flower of grass.
The word of the Lord endures for ever.
The grass withers, and the flower falls.
The word of the Lord endures for ever.
That word is the good news that was announced to you.
The word of the Lord endures for ever.

ISAIAH 40:1, 6-8 AND 1 PETER 1:24-25

Almighty God,
in Christ you make all things new:
transform the poverty of our nature by the riches of your grace,
and in the renewal of our lives
make known your heavenly glory;
through Jesus Christ your Son our Lord,
who is alive and reigns with you,
in the unity of the Holy Spirit,
one God, now and for ever.
Amen.

Conversation

How do you feel about the Bible? Is it something that excites you? Fills you with dread? Inspires you? Makes you feel guilty?

Do you think it is relevant or irrelevant in our modern world? Talk about this in your group.

Reflecting on Scripture

Reading

Then Jesus, filled with the power of the Spirit, returned to Galilee, and a report about him spread through all the surrounding country. [15]He began to teach in their synagogues and was praised by everyone. [16]When he came to Nazareth, where he had been brought up, he went to the synagogue on the sabbath day, as was his custom. He stood up to read, [17]and the scroll of the prophet Isaiah was given to him. He unrolled the scroll and found the place where it was written:
[18]"The Spirit of the Lord is upon me, because he has anointed me to bring good news to the poor. He has sent me to proclaim release to the captives and recovery of sight to the blind, to let the oppressed go free, [19]to proclaim the year of the Lord's favor."
[20]And he rolled up the scroll, gave it back to the attendant, and sat down. The eyes of all in the synagogue were fixed on him. [21]Then he began to say to them, "Today this scripture has been fulfilled in your hearing."
[22]All spoke well of him and were amazed at the gracious words that came from his mouth. They said, "Is not this Joseph's son?"

LUKE 4:14-22

Explanatory note

In synagogues it was the custom to read one reading from the Torah and one from the Prophets. They would then discuss the readings together. What Jesus did in the synagogue at Nazareth seems to have been a natural part of what would have taken place in the synagogue.

Jesus read from what we would now call Isaiah 61:1-2, though not from the whole passage—you might like to look and see what is missing from what he read.

● Read the passage through once.

● Keep a few moments' silence.

● Read the passage a second time with different voices.

- Invite everyone to say aloud a word or phrase that strikes them.
- Read the passage a third time.
- Share together what this word or phrase might mean and what questions it raises.

Reflection   PAULA GOODER

The Bible as library

The encouragement to read your Bible appears simple and straightforward. In the English-speaking world we are blessed with many different English translations. So, surely, all that is necessary is that you pick the one you like and off you go?

Anyone who has tried this will tell you that it won't be long before you hit problems. The further into the Bible you get from Genesis the harder the going gets. Some people succeed and reach the end, but many give up and from then on struggle to read it at all. Part of the problem is that many people treat the Bible as though it is a novel: easy to read, chronological and sequential or, failing that, as though it is an encyclopedia (annoyingly organized out of alphabetical order) into which you can dip to find answers to a range of questions. It is neither of these.

> The Bible is a collection of 66 books.

Contrary to its title "The Bible," which implies that it is a single volume, the Bible is in fact a collection of 66 books, 39 in the Old Testament, 27 in the New Testament, many written by different authors, at different times, and in different places. This is reflected much more accurately by its Greek title "Ta Biblia," which means "the books." Just as you would no more enter a library or bookshop and read the first book you come across followed by the ones next to it on the shelf, so there is no reason why you should read the books in the order in which you find them in the Bible. It is a mix of different types of writing (law, history, poetry, wisdom, letters, biography, and so on) and it can help to know what type of book you are about to read before you begin.

For discussion

- Do you read the Bible? If yes, share with the group how you read it. All the way through? In small chunks? Do you listen to an audio version or have you watched films based on it? What has worked best for you?

- Does thinking about the Bible as a collection of books or as a library help in any way?

The Story of salvation

Once we realize that the Bible is not a single book designed to be read from beginning to end, it is, intriguingly, easier to see it as a whole. The books were not written chronologically, nor are they now arranged chronologically. Indeed, especially in the prophetic books, you can jump time periods by as much as a couple of hundred years from book to book. But if you step back and look at the Bible as a whole, it tells the story of the relationship between God and the world from the dawn of time (in Genesis) until its ending (in the book of Revelation).

Over the years there have been huge arguments about what the Bible is. Most recently the Bible's scientific credibility and historical reliability in particular have been challenged. It is important to recognize,

The Bible tells the story of God's love for the human race.

however, what the Bible is and what it is not. It is neither a scientific textbook nor even a newspaper article, and so cannot be evaluated as though it is. As we've already observed, it contains many different types of material, from law to poetry, biography to visions, which are all discussing and reflecting on God and God's relationship with humanity.

As we trace this story through, it becomes clear that the major story that returns again and again in all the different types of writing is the story of God's love for the human race: a love that continues despite humanity's arrogance and evil; a love that eventually led God to send God's own Son to die. This is not a story that begins on page 1 and ends on its final page but is a golden thread that runs through the whole Bible and is expressed in poetry, law, story, and song.

Some people describe the Bible as a five-act play in which the final half act is not written down. The first act is the story of creation, and the second the fall. The third act is the story of Israel and God's first covenants with the people. The fourth act introduces us to the story of Jesus and his death and resurrection, and the fifth to the story of Christians and the Christian Church. So on this model the Bible contains the first four acts and the opening of the fifth act (The Acts of the Apostles). Our task as Christians is to read these first four and a half acts and then carry on the story in our lives.

God's grand play of love is not yet complete and we are called to take our parts in that play. The Bible, giving as it does the first four and a half acts of the play, sets our course. We read the Bible so that we learn more about how the play began, and we listen for the director's instructions as we play our part. The Bible is not just a book to read. It is a book to live.

> **In short**
>
> The Bible tells the story of the expression of God's love in the world, a love that caused God to send God's Son to die for us. As we live our lives, we continue that story of God's love in the world.

For discussion

- How have you experienced the story of God's love in your own life?
- What role, if any, should the Bible have in modern discussions about science?
- What would it mean for how we live our lives to take seriously a call to continue living the fifth act of God's five-act play of love?

Journeying On

We would encourage you to reflect on one of these six verses from the Bible each day between the sessions. Read it, pray about it, listen to what God might be saying to you in it, and allow it to change you.

For the word of the LORD is upright, and all his work is done in faithfulness (Psalm 33:4).

In God, whose word I praise, in the LORD, whose word I praise, in God I trust; I am not afraid (Psalm 56:10-11).

For God so loved the world that he gave his only Son, so that everyone who believes in him may not perish but may have eternal life (John 3:16).

How precious is your steadfast love, O God! All people may take refuge in the shadow of your wings (Psalm 36:7).

For I am convinced that neither death, nor life, nor angels, nor rulers, nor things present, nor things to come, nor powers, nor height, nor depth, nor anything else in all creation, will be able to separate us from the love of God in Christ Jesus our Lord (Romans 8:38-39).

The grace of the Lord Jesus Christ, the love of God, and the communion of the Holy Spirit be with all of you (2 Corinthians 13:13).

Concluding Prayers

God of love,
the Bible recounts the story
of your great love poured out on us.
Help us to live out that story of love
every day of our lives
in everything that we say and do.
Amen.

As our Savior taught us, so we pray,
Our Father... (see pp. 5-6)

Wisdom for the Journey

Lord, who can comprehend even one of your words? We lose more of it than we grasp, like those who drink from a living spring. For God's word offers different facets according to the capacity of the listener, and the Lord has portrayed his message in many colors, so that whoever gazes upon it can see in it what suits. Within it God has buried a variety of treasures, so that each of us might grow rich in seeking them out.

EPHREM OF SYRIA (C. 306-73)

If you wish to secure a true knowledge of Scripture you must first nurture within yourself humility of heart which is unshakable. Only this will ensure that your knowledge does not puff you up, but instead illuminates your heart through love.

JOHN CASSIAN (C. 360-435)

If we want to be always in God's company, we must pray regularly and read the Scriptures regularly. When we pray, we talk to God; when we read, God talks to us.

ISIDORE OF SEVILLE (C. 560-636)

It is important to spend time in the systematic reading of Scripture. For if you read now here, now there, the various things that chance and circumstance cause you to stumble across, it will not consolidate your learning. For it is easy to take such reading in, and easier still to forget it. You should also pause over certain authors and allow yourself to become accustomed to their style. For it is important to read the Scriptures in the same spirit in which they were written because only in that spirit are they to be understood.

GUIGO V (1083-1136)

The Bible is a vast web of interwoven conversations, encounters of faith and struggle and disclosure between God and men and women. As we become familiar with them we find ourselves drawn into more and more of them. In prayer I put myself into one of those conversations and God uses the historic faith encounter to draw me into my own today.

MARTIN L. SMITH (1947-)

THE BIBLE AS BREATH

pilgrim

In this session we are reflecting on what it means to say that the Bible is the breath of God.

Opening Prayers

But the steadfast love of the LORD is from
everlasting to everlasting on those who fear him,
May your word inspire us, O Lord,
and his righteousness to children's children,
May your word inspire us, O Lord,
to those who keep his covenant
May your word inspire us, O Lord,
and remember to do his commandments.
May your word inspire us, O Lord.
The LORD has established his throne in the heavens,
May your word inspire us, O Lord,
and his kingdom rules over all.
May your word inspire us, O Lord.
Bless the LORD, O you his angels,
May your word inspire us, O Lord,
you mighty ones who do his bidding, obedient to his spoken word.
May your word inspire us, O Lord.

PSALM 103:17-21

Almighty God,
in the birth of your Son
you have poured on us the new light of your incarnate Word,
and shown us the fullness of your love:
help us to walk in his light and dwell in his love
that we may know the fullness of his joy;
who is alive and reigns with you,
in the unity of the Holy Spirit,
one God, now and for ever.
Amen.

Conversation

**Share with the group any reflections you have had on the Bible
verses you were thinking about from the Journeying On section last
week.**

Take a moment to sit quietly, take a deep breath in and let it out slowly. Notice what the breath feels like. Discuss "breath"—what words spring to mind in connection with breath (such as life, vitality, and so on)?

Reflecting on Scripture

Reading

But as for you, continue in what you have learned and firmly believed, knowing from whom you learned it, [15]and how from childhood you have known the sacred writings that are able to instruct you for salvation through faith in Christ Jesus. [16]All scripture is inspired by God and is useful for teaching, for reproof, for correction, and for training in righteousness, [17]so that everyone who belongs to God may be proficient, equipped for every good work.

2 TIMOTHY 3:14-17

Explanatory note

2 Timothy is addressed, as you might expect, to "Timothy." If this Timothy is the same person referred to in Acts, then we know that his mother was Jewish and his father a Gentile. As a result he would have learned the Bible from an early age.

The word translated "inspired by God" is a slightly odd word made up of two separate words—the word for God and a word connected to "breathed," so means literally "God breathed."

- Read the passage through once.

- Keep a few moments' silence.

- Read the passage a second time with different voices.

- Invite everyone to say aloud a word or phrase that strikes them.

- Read the passage a third time.

- Share together what this word or phrase might mean and what questions it raises.

The Word as the breath of God

As 2 Timothy illustrates, Christians see the Bible as "inspired by God." If we take the word "inspire" seriously we can say that this means that the authors of the Bible were animated by an in-breathing, a breathing in of the life-giving and creative Word of God like an inhalation of fresh air. The oxygenation, the new life and enrichment that inhalation gives through the lungs within a living person, is comparable to the breathing of new life into our whole being when we are blessed by the words of sacred Scripture. By this inspiration, we make deeper and deeper discoveries about God within us and the world, and more and more fresh expressions of the life-giving Word that sustains and creates the world all the time.

> The Bible is a prayerful collection of words about Jesus.

The Bible is a prayerful collection of words about Jesus, the Word of God as he is called at the start of that Gospel. As the prologue to John's Gospel puts it so poetically, the Word of God has been present with God since the dawn of time and with God has created everything that lives and breathes in all creation. The Word of God is what became incarnate in Jesus of Nazareth's life, teaching, death, and resurrection. Jesus Christ is the living Word of God, in the flesh, in our world, and in our lives. The Bible witnesses to Jesus as this Word of God, one way or another: anticipating, echoing, approaching, describing, hallowing, depicting, and witnessing to the Christ.

So the Bible is the written word of God, which witnesses to the living Word of God, Jesus Christ. The Word of God is not black print on a white page; the Word of God is a person, who is represented in the books of the Bible. This crucial point helps us to understand the Bible as the Breath of God. Jesus in the Gospels breathes the Holy Spirit; he is the Word incarnate, God with us, God for us, one of us yet from the heart of God.

This way of seeing the Bible as an expression of the breath of God, incarnate in Jesus, becomes crucial when we come to interpret and use the Bible for meaning and purpose in our lives. It means that when we read the black print on the white page, we approach it with great prayer, care, and respect as an authority for us, in that it points to or reveals Jesus the Christ, the living Word of God.

> **In short**
> The Bible is the written word of God that bears witness to the living Word of God, Jesus Christ, and we see the Bible as the breath of God.

For discussion

- When do you feel most inspired in life? Share an experience when you have felt great inspiration and talk about why it was so inspiring.

- What do *you* think it means to say that the Bible is the word of God?  *required by God through people*

- Have you ever found yourself inspired when reading the Bible? Which passages have most inspired you and why?

The Bible as a house *2 Creation Stories*

What we are aiming for in our reading of the Bible is a deep engagement and fresh discovery that is a process of living in and living out the word of God. It can be compared to entering a large house with many rooms.

First, as you approach the house you see the front of the building with its dimensions, structure, and doorway. This may be compared to encountering and approaching the black print on the white paper.

Second, you enter the door. This is like entering a chapter of the Bible. You stand inside the spacious house and take off your shoes because you are standing on holy ground. In other words, you place yourself within the book concerned and pray as you read.

Third, around you are the walls of each room. The walls on one side may be compared to the context in which each book is written; the walls on the other side to the context in which you live. You need both the question of what inspired the author to write as they did and the question of what it says in our current context for the house to stand.

Finally, there is the roof of the house, which can be compared to the canopy that the Church provides. It encompasses all the rooms, covering the entire sacred space and providing the shelter and the live-ability of the experience. The Bible is the Church's book; it was put together as we now have it by an overarching canonical process of church discernment about what was true to the word of God. Reading and interpreting the Bible is best done within a church community of shared discernment and community wisdom.

You need all four dimensions of this house, this biblical encounter, to live, to read the Bible holistically and authentically. Reading and interpreting the Bible is a four-dimensional process; miss any one of these and you are diminished in your biblical experience, like only filling your lungs half full of fresh air, for example.

Breathe in, breathe deep, and feel the invigoration of the breath of God through the inspiration of the word of God in your being. It makes all the difference to your walk with God in the world.

In short

Imagine a house. The front of the house is the actual words of the Bible; reading a chapter of the Bible is like entering a room. The walls of the room are the authors' context and your own context that you bring to the Bible. The roof is the Church that provides shelter for the whole house.

For discussion

- Spend some time talking about the image of the Bible as a house. What is helpful about that image for understanding it better? Was there anything you found offputting about it?

- Are there any of the four aspects of the house that you find more difficult than others?

- Do you agree that the Bible is best read together in a community?

Journeying On

Here are some verses from the Bible to reflect on this week, one each for six days:

Then the LORD God formed man from the dust of the ground, and breathed into his nostrils the breath of life; and the man became a living being (Genesis 2:7).

Just as you do not know how the breath comes to the bones in the mother's womb, so you do not know the work of God, who makes everything (Ecclesiastes 11:5).

I will put my spirit within you, and you shall live (Ezekiel 37:14).

The wind blows where it chooses, and you hear the sound of it, but you do not know where it comes from or where it goes. So it is with everyone who is born of the Spirit (John 3:8).

If the Spirit of him who raised Jesus from the dead dwells in you, he who raised Christ from the dead will give life to your mortal bodies also through his Spirit that dwells in you (Romans 8:11).

Now the Lord is the Spirit, and where the Spirit of the Lord is, there is freedom (2 Corinthians 3:17).

Concluding Prayers

God of life,
your breath brings new life into the world
fill us with your life-giving Spirit
through our reading of your word
so that inspired by it
we may be transformed into the likeness
of your Son Jesus Christ, the living Word.
Amen.

As our Savior taught us, so we pray, **Our Father...** (see pp. 5-6)

Wisdom for the Journey

In a psalm, instruction vies with beauty. We sing for pleasure. We learn for profit.

AMBROSE OF MILAN (C. 334-97)

Read the holy Scriptures constantly. Indeed never let the sacred volume be out of your hand. Learn what you have to teach, and as Scripture says: "Be ready to give an answer to anyone who asks you to give a reason for the hope that is in you."

JEROME (C. 342-420)

Learning unsupported by grace may get into our ears, but it will never reach the heart. It makes a great noise outside but serves no inner purpose. But when God's grace touches our innermost minds to bring understanding, his Word which has been received by the ear sinks deep into the heart.

ISIDORE OF SEVILLE (C. 560-636)

Give diligence, reader, that thou come with a pure mind, and as Scripture saith, with a single eye unto the words of health and of eternal life by the which, if we repent and believe them, we are born anew and created afresh.

WILLIAM TYNDALE (1494-1536)

THE BIBLE AS A STREAM OF LIVING WATER

pilgrim ───────────────────────────

In this session we are exploring how the Bible nourishes us.

Redemption ~ whole concept of Bible

Opening Prayers

The law of the LORD is perfect, reviving the soul;
Nourish us with your word, O Lord,
the decrees of the LORD are sure, making wise the simple;
Nourish us with your word, O Lord,
the precepts of the LORD are right, rejoicing the heart;
Nourish us with your word, O Lord,
the commandment of the LORD is clear, enlightening the eyes;
Nourish us with your word, O Lord,
the fear of the LORD is pure, enduring for ever;
Nourish us with your word, O Lord,
the ordinances of the LORD are true and righteous altogether.
More to be desired are they than gold, even much fine gold;
Nourish us with your word, O Lord,
sweeter also than honey, and drippings of the honeycomb.

PSALM 19:7-10

God of glory,
you nourish us with your Word
who is the bread of life:
fill us with your Holy Spirit
that through us the light of your glory
may shine in all the world.
We ask this in the name of Jesus Christ our Lord.
Amen.

Conversation

Share with the group any reflections you have had on the Bible verses you were thinking about from the Journeying On section last week.

What nourishes you, physically, emotionally, and spiritually, in your everyday life?

Reflecting on Scripture

[handwritten: instead of people denying you]

Reading

[handwritten: when people or talk ness — "say let us pray"]

Happy are those who do not follow the advice of the wicked,
or take the path that sinners tread, or sit in the seat of scoffers;
²but their delight is in the law of the LORD,
and on his law they meditate day and night.
³They are like trees planted by streams of water,
which yield their fruit in its season, and their leaves do not
wither. In all that they do, they prosper.
⁴The wicked are not so,
but are like chaff that the wind drives away.
⁵Therefore the wicked will not stand in the judgement,
nor sinners in the congregation of the righteous;
⁶for the LORD watches over the way of the righteous,
but the way of the wicked will perish.

PSALM 1

Explanatory note

The word translated "happy" here has a range of possible meaning, from "blessed" to "fortunate" to "happy." The idea is that people are happy because they are blessed. This kind of idea is picked up by Jesus in the Beatitudes, which are more often translated as "blessed."

The law of the Lord referred to here is the Torah, or the first five books of the Bible, so it is talking about those whose delight is in the Bible.

- Read the passage through once.
- Keep a few moments' silence.
- Read the passage a second time with different voices.
- Invite everyone to say aloud a word or phrase that strikes them.
- Read the passage a third time.
- Share together what this word or phrase might mean and what questions it raises.

Reflection
(handwritten: spiritual life source · ① pray ② the word and the ... → flourish)

ROSEMARY LAIN-PRIESTLEY

A balanced diet

The writer of Psalm 1 tells us that those who attend to God's word in the Bible will flourish and thrive because: "They are like trees planted by streams of living water, which yield their fruit in its season, and their leaves do not wither."

> The Bible as we have received it is a rich mix.
> *(handwritten: How many souls ... did you ... to spread the word ... the Bible)*

The Bible as we have received it is a rich mix of history, poetry, epic writings, wise sayings, letters, gospel, mystical visions, and so much more. Its span and variety are breathtaking; those who look for God's guidance here will be inspired and challenged, sometimes confused or surprised, and always encouraged to explore further.

On the banks of this deep and refreshing stream the ground is steeped in the nutrients that, season after season, will encourage us to grow and be renewed. As our roots push deeper we will grow in our understanding of ourselves, others, God, and the world.

For the healthy growth of our bodies we need a balanced diet incorporating a range of nutrients. In the same way our growing understanding of God will flourish best if we are prepared to explore the length and breadth of the Scriptures. Confining our reading to the Gospels, or the Old Testament, or Paul's letters will lead to spiritual growth that is uneven and lopsided.

Some churches encourage us to range far and wide in our exploration of the Bible by providing a structured framework known as a lectionary, a list of readings to be used in worship over a period of time. Others offer sermons, talks, and Bible studies based on a series of themes. On our own, we can use Bible reading notes to guide us across a range of biblical material. In these ways we are encouraged to explore beyond our favorite passages to material that is fresh and challenging for us.

> **In short**
>
> The Bible provides us with a rich diet of nourishment for our Christian journey. It is important to ensure that we avail ourselves of the full range of spiritual nourishment offered in the Bible.

For discussion

- Which parts of the Bible do you read the most? Why do you gravitate more to them than to others? Which parts of the Bible do you read the least? Why do you avoid them?

- What "nutrients" do you think you might be missing in your encounters with the Bible?

PS: It may be that you haven't yet had the time or the opportunity to read the Bible much at all. If so, don't be embarrassed! You might know some of the stories and you can talk about which are your favorites!

A lifetime's exploration

Paul explained to the early Christian believers in the church at Corinth that the spiritual teaching he offered them was tailored to what they needed and could use at the time. "I fed you with milk, not solid food, for you were not ready for solid food" (1 Corinthians 3:2). Paul adapted the depth and content of his teaching according to the needs of his hearers.

Similarly, what we need to hear and learn will change in the various seasons of our lives, and so at different times we will turn to particular passages, books, or even genres to find what most connects with our situation. This could depend on our age and stage of life. The call of Jeremiah (Jeremiah 1:4-10) or Paul's words to Timothy (1 Timothy 4:12) can offer confidence to those who are feeling uncertain of themselves at an early stage in life. In the shifting sands of middle age we might find solid ground in the wisdom writings of Ecclesiastes and Proverbs.

Older people may experience a keen shift in perspective that finds them delving into passages that resonate with the wisdom of their experience and the constancy of God's love that will steady them as endings become more frequent and imminent.

What we need to hear and learn will change in the various seasons of our lives.

Across the span of our human journey there will be numerous experiences planned and unplanned, longed for and dreaded. There will be failures and embarrassments, achievements and lovely surprises. In times of sorrow we might turn to the comfort of certain Psalms; when we're angry, Job's outraged rant against God and the universe can be a therapeutic read; the stories of Jesus' encounters with those on the margins will resonate if we're feeling excluded or lonely. In each different time and season the Scriptures have something to offer: if we don't find easy and direct answers to our questions, there will be clues and nuggets of comfort, wisdom, or encouragement.

There is no quick win when it comes to acquiring familiarity with the Bible. Those who can instinctively turn to the appropriate passage for the occasion have invariably learned that ability over many years of reading, meditation, and prayer. But any one of us can begin to put down roots in the Scriptures right here and now.

Establishing our roots in the water of this living stream is not a task with a finite deadline. Rather, it is a lifetime's epic adventure that, given time and attention, will connect with every aspect of our lives and reflect the risks and riches, the frustrations and sudden joys of our human experience in God's world.

In short

Becoming rooted in the Bible with all it has to teach us is a lifetime's task, and as we go through life we will find that different parts of the Bible speak to us.

For discussion

- How easy do you find reading the Bible? If you do read it, share with the group how you go about doing so. If not, talk about what puts you off.

- If you have known (or known of) the stories of the Bible for a while, are you aware that your tastes have changed? Are there bits you like now that you did not used to like, or bits you used to find helpful that now are less helpful?

Journeying On

Here are some verses from the Bible to reflect on this week, one each for six days:

For my people have committed two evils: they have forsaken me, the fountain of living water, and dug out cisterns for themselves, cracked cisterns that can hold no water (Jeremiah 2:13).

I would feed you with the finest of the wheat, and with honey from the rock I would satisfy you (Psalm 81:16).

Remove far from me falsehood and lying; give me neither poverty nor riches; feed me with the food that I need (Proverbs 30:8).

Give us this day our daily bread (Matthew 6:11).

Jesus said to them, "I am the bread of life. Whoever comes to me will never be hungry, and whoever believes in me will never be thirsty" (John 6:35).

On the last day of the festival, the great day, while Jesus was standing there, he cried out, "Let anyone who is thirsty come to me, and let the one who believes in me drink" (John 7:37-38).

Concluding Prayers

God of all nourishment,
teach us to sink our roots deep into your word
that nourished by your wisdom
we might find ourselves held steadfast
in your truth and love.
Amen.

As our Savior taught us, so we pray, **Our Father...** (see pp. 5-6)

Wisdom for the Journey

Let us invite Christ to dig out our well, to clear out the earth, and
cleanse it of impurity. In spite of any accumulated pollution, we
shall discover there living water, water of which the Lord says:
"Those who believe in me, out of their belly shall flow streams
of living water." For the Word of God is present within us, and
his work is to remove the earth from the soul of each of us, to let
the springs of water within gush free, for "the kingdom of God is
within you."

ORIGEN (C. 185–C. 254)

Jesus Christ is the fountain of life and he invites us to drink deep.
Whoever loves him, drinks him. You drink who are filled with the
Word of God. You drink who love him fully and really desire him.
You drink who are on fire with the love of wisdom.

COLUMBANUS (C. 543–615)

Think of the word of God in the way you think of your food.
When bread is kept in a bin, a thief can steal it or a mouse can find
its way in and nibble it. Eventually, of course, it goes stale. In the
same way, treasure the word of God because those who keep it are
blessed. Feed on it, digest it, allow its goodness to pass into your
body so that your affections and whole behavior is nourished and
transformed. Do not forget to eat your bread and your heart will
not wither. Fill your soul with God's richness and strength.

BERNARD OF CLAIRVAUX (1090-1153)

THE BIBLE AS A LAMP

pilgrim

undistractably
not enlarging
in exhaustible

In this session we think about the Bible as something that enlightens and informs us as Christians.

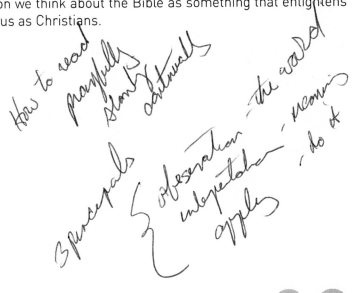

How to read
prayerfully
slowly
attentively

3 principals

observation — the world
interpretation — meaning
apply — do it

Opening Prayers

Let your steadfast love become my comfort according to your promise
to your servant.
Your word is a light to my path.
Let your mercy come to me, that I may live; for your law is my delight.
Your word is a light to my path.
Let the arrogant be put to shame, because they have subverted me
with guile;
Your word is a light to my path.
as for me, I will meditate on your precepts.
Your word is a light to my path.
Let those who fear you turn to me, so that they may know your
decrees.
Your word is a light to my path.
May my heart be blameless in your statutes, so that I may not be put
to shame.
Your word is a light to my path.
My soul languishes for your salvation; I hope in your word.
Your word is a light to my path.

PSALM 119:76-81

Almighty God,
We thank you for the gift of your holy word.
May it be a lantern to our feet
A light upon our paths
And a strength to our lives.
Take us and use us
To love and serve all people
In the power of the Holy Spirit
And in the name of your Son
Jesus Christ our Lord.
Amen.

Conversation

Share with the group any reflections you have had on the Bible verses you were thinking about from the Journeying On section last week.

Share with the group any examples of people, events, or writings that have shed light in your life.

Reflecting on Scripture

Reading

Oh, how I love your law! It is my meditation all day long.
[98]Your commandment makes me wiser than my enemies, for it is always with me.
[99]I have more understanding than all my teachers, for your decrees are my meditation.
[100]I understand more than the aged, for I keep your precepts.
[101]I hold back my feet from every evil way, in order to keep your word.
[102]I do not turn away from your ordinances, for you have taught me.
[103]How sweet are your words to my taste, sweeter than honey to my mouth!
[104]Through your precepts I get understanding; therefore I hate every false way.
[105]Your word is a lamp to my feet and a light to my path.
[106]I have sworn an oath and confirmed it, to observe your righteous ordinances.
[107]I am severely afflicted; give me life, O LORD, according to your word.
[108]Accept my offerings of praise, O LORD, and teach me your ordinances.
[109]I hold my life in my hand continually, but I do not forget your law.
[110]The wicked have laid a snare for me, but I do not stray from your precepts.

[111]Your decrees are my heritage for ever; they are the joy of my heart.
[112]I incline my heart to perform your statutes for ever, to the end.

PSALM 119:97-112

Explanatory note

As with Psalm 1, the law referred to here is the Torah, the first five books of the Bible. References to "The Law" are probably to the whole Torah; the words "decrees" and "statutes" refer more to the individual commands within the whole Torah.

● Read the passage through once.

● Keep a few moments' silence.

● Read the passage a second time with different voices.

● Invite everyone to say aloud a word or phrase that strikes them.

● Read the passage a third time.

● Share together what this word or phrase might mean and what questions it raises.

Reflection
VIVIENNE FAULL

A story that forms us

Each of us lives by a story, perhaps one that has been chosen for us or one we have chosen for ourselves. It may not be very coherent or conscious, and may only emerge when we try to find ways to bring up our children, run a business or lead a community when we hear ourselves saying: "'Mom used to...", "My boss once said...", or "My wise friend taught me..." The story is what shapes who we are and how we live.

The Bible did not spring fully formed into existence.

Christians are people whose story is formed by the Bible and who have learned who they are and how they should live by reading and learning from the stories of Scripture, from that wealth of writings that was forged through years of reflection on people's experience of God's work in the world. The Bible did not spring fully formed into existence. Instead these writings were assembled by the people of Israel over many centuries. What we now call the Old Testament is made up of three main collections:

- the Torah, the first five books of the Bible, which as well as law, contains many important stories about the origins of Israel;
- the Prophets, which contains books that we might call historical, like 1 and 2 Samuel and 1 and 2 Kings, as well as the prophecies of people like Isaiah;
- the Writings, which contains a wide variety of different kinds of books, from the Psalms to the book of Esther.

Each of these collections was gathered together slowly, the Torah probably reaching its final form first and the Writings last. Even at the time of Jesus the details of what should be included in the tradition was still disputed. Jesus talked regularly about the law and the Prophets (the first two collections of books) but less often about the Writings or the books it contained. A similarly dynamic process created the New Testament. Like the Old Testament it was gathered together slowly over time as the earliest Christian communities discerned together which of the earliest writings were sacred. Contrary to some popular opinion, the decision to include some texts and not others was not arbitrary and imposed by a few people but emerged through general agreement between different communities of Christians. Like a work of art, the Hebrew and Christian Scriptures were worked and reworked until their form and content was recognized to be complete and authoritative.

> **In short**
> Christians are people whose story is formed by the Bible. We read it so that our lives might be formed by it.

A story that sheds light for us

Christians inherited from the people of Israel a sense of Scripture being powerful and formative not only for disciples but for the whole world. That is why biblical texts are at the heart of church life, used extensively in reading and song, and used as a source for teaching. Christians also inherited from the people of Israel a sense that Scripture is significant as a reminder of who we are and should be.

This story that forms us is an ancient story that spans hundreds and thousands of years. It is a story that tells us who God was, is, and will be. It is a story that tells us who we are, as descendants of God's people. Like the author of Psalm 119, Christians today still believe that God's word is a lamp to our feet and a light to our path. Unlike the author of Psalm 119, Christians no longer see the law, alone, as showing us the way. We now look to the whole Bible for illumination about the path we should take. The whole Bible—from the laws to the stories, from the poetry to the letters, from the wisdom sayings to the Gospels—sheds light for us on our lives and the way we should take.

> *Biblical texts are at the heart of church life.*

This does not mean that the Bible offers us easy answers. It does not contain a mechanistic, mathematical formula into which you program your question and an answer appears. Instead it sheds light. It tells stories of what happened when people went this way rather than that way. It tells God's messages over time to people showing them the best that they could be and do. When we take the whole Bible together we can begin to perceive a persistent light that shines, urging us to act with justice and mercy, to love God and our neighbors, and to fashion our lives around Christ in everything that we say and do.

> **In short**
> Christians believe that the whole Bible—from Genesis to Revelation—sheds light on our path, helping us to see which way to go.

For discussion

- Which parts of the Bible do you think light your way? Which bar your way? Why?

- The problem, of course, is that Christians don't always agree about the light that the Bible shines on our path. Discuss some examples of this and talk about what issues arise when this kind of disagreement happens.

- Recall an occasion when the Bible has particularly shone light for you or for someone you know.

Journeying On

Here are some verses from the Bible to reflect on this week, one each for six days:

The LORD bless you and keep you; the LORD make his face to shine upon you, and be gracious to you; the LORD lift up his countenance upon you, and give you peace (Numbers 6:24-26).

O, that I were as in the months of old, as in the days when God watched over me; when his lamp shone over my head, and by his light I walked through darkness (Job 29:2-3).

But the path of the righteous is like the light of dawn, which shines brighter and brighter until full day (Proverbs 4:18).

The sun shall no longer be your light by day, nor for brightness shall the moon give light to you by night; but the LORD will be your everlasting light, and your God will be your glory (Isaiah 60:19).

The light shines in the darkness, and the darkness did not overcome it (John 1:5).

For it is the God who said, "Let light shine out of darkness," who has shone in our hearts to give the light of the knowledge of the glory of God in the face of Jesus Christ (2 Corinthians 4:6).

Concluding Prayers

God of all light,
illumine us with your wisdom:
show us which path to take,
bring us ever nearer to the
glorious light that shines in the face
of your Son, Jesus Christ.
Amen.

As our Savior taught us, so we pray,
Our Father... (see pp. 5-6)

Wisdom for the Journey

All spiritual growth comes from reading and reflection. By reading God's Word we learn what we did not know; by reflecting on it we retain what we have learned.

EPHREM OF SYRIA (C. 306-73)

The psalms are the bright mirror in which we become more profoundly conscious of what is happening to us in our lives. We are made sensitive by our own experience. It is no longer a question of second-hand knowledge. We are in touch with reality. Their meaning is not like something entrusted to our memory but rather, something we give birth to in the depths of our heart through an intuition that forms part of our being. We enter into their meaning not because of what we have read but because of what we have ourselves experienced.

JOHN CASSIAN (C. 360-435)

Dear friends, what can be more delightful than this voice of the Lord inviting us? Behold, in his loving mercy, the Lord is showing us the way of life. Clothed with faith and the performance of good works, and with the gospel as our guide, let us set out on this way of life that we may deserve to see the God who is calling us into his kingdom.

BENEDICT (480-550)

Never approach the words of the mysteries that are contained in Scripture without praying and asking God for help. Say, "Lord, let me feel the power that is in them." Prayer is the key that opens the true meaning of the Scriptures.

ISAAC OF NINEVEH (7TH CENTURY)

Let no day pass without reading some portion of the Holy Scripture. If you can, let this course of reading follow the course of the psalms, or of some other lessons, according to the Prayer Book.

It is good to acquire the habit of reading the New Testament for devotion in Greek when you can do it with ease, by which much is learned that the English translation of necessity leaves in the shade.

WILLIAM EWART GLADSTONE (1809–98)

It is not possible to develop the capacity to see beauty without developing also the capacity to see ugliness, for they are the same capacity. The capacity for joy is also the capacity for pain. We soon find that any increase in our sensitiveness to what is lovely in the world increases also our capacity for being hurt.

JOHN MACMURRAY (1891–1976)

SESSION FIVE:
THE BIBLE AS A TWO-EDGED SWORD

pilgrim

In this session we ask what it means to say that the Bible is living
and active.

Opening Prayers

Sing to him a new song; play skillfully on the strings, with loud shouts.
We hope in your word.
For the word of the LORD is upright, and all his work is done in faithfulness.
We hope in your word.
He loves righteousness and justice; the earth is full of the steadfast love of the LORD.
We hope in your word.
By the word of the LORD the heavens were made, and all their host by the breath of his mouth.
We hope in your word.
He gathered the waters of the sea as in a bottle; he put the deeps in storehouses.
We hope in your word.
Let all the earth fear the LORD; let all the inhabitants of the world stand in awe of him.
We hope in your word.
For he spoke, and it came to be; he commanded, and it stood firm.
We hope in your word.

PSALM 33:3-9

Almighty God,
you have created the heavens and the earth
and made us in your own image:
teach us to discern your hand in all your works
and your likeness in all your children;
through Jesus Christ your Son our Lord,
who with you and the Holy Spirit reigns supreme over all things,
now and for ever.
Amen.

Conversation

Share with the group any reflections you have had on the Bible verses you were thinking about from the Journeying On section last week.

The word "discernment" can feel vague and hard to tie down. What does it mean to you?

Reflecting on Scripture

Reading

Indeed, the word of God is living and active, sharper than any two-edged sword, piercing until it divides soul from spirit, joints from marrow; it is able to judge the thoughts and intentions of the heart. ¹³And before him no creature is hidden, but all are naked and laid bare to the eyes of the one to whom we must render an account. ¹⁴Since, then, we have a great high priest who has passed through the heavens, Jesus, the Son of God, let us hold fast to our confession. ¹⁵For we do not have a high priest who is unable to sympathize with our weaknesses, but we have one who in every respect has been tested as we are, yet without sin. ¹⁶Let us therefore approach the throne of grace with boldness, so that we may receive mercy and find grace to help in time of need.

HEBREWS 4:12-16

Explanatory note

The reference to the "high priest" in this passage refers to the Jewish Temple in Jerusalem. Once a year the high priest would enter the "Holy of Holies," the most sacred part of the Temple which, they believed, opened directly into heaven itself. The Letter to the Hebrews sees Jesus as a high priest whose death has done away with the need for a temple and who, himself, intercedes directly with God on our behalf. The throne of Grace is a reference to God's throne in heaven, which in biblical tradition is the place from which all grace flows.

- Read the passage through once.
- Keep a few moments' silence.
- Read the passage a second time with different voices.
- Invite everyone to say aloud a word or phrase that strikes them.
- Read the passage a third time.
- Share together what this word or phrase might mean and what questions it raises.

Reflection   PAULA GOODER

The living, active word of God

It is very easy to slip into treating the Bible as though it is a passive object, a "thing." We read the Bible. We interpret the Bible. We quote the Bible. We love the Bible. But in all of these the Bible is an object and the implication is that we are the active agents in what is going on. Hebrews 4:12 suggests otherwise. "The word of God," it declares, "is living and active."

As the passage goes on it becomes clear that, as we noticed in Session 2, there is a strong overlap between the *written* word of God (the Scriptures) and the *incarnated* Word of God (Jesus). The verses before this passage contain references to characters from the Old Testament, but the verses following verse 12 begin to describe the word of God as "he" and "him." Indeed verse 14 talks about the word of God being a great high priest. In the space of a few verses the author makes clear that the Word of God refers *both* to the Scriptures and to the person they point to—Jesus.

The Scriptures live and are active.

No wonder then that it/he is living and active. Just as Jesus is vibrantly alive, so also the Scriptures live and are active. Many Christians who read the Bible regularly would recognize this description. One of the most remarkable features of regular, deep engagement with the Scriptures is a growing sense that it is not so much we who read the Bible, but the Bible that reads us. It doesn't happen straightaway, but over time it becomes increasingly clear that the Bible can reveal to us who we really are. It can speak deep within us to our often unconscious fears and desires. It can draw us inexorably closer to God. Deep, engaged reading of the Bible is a dynamic process that transforms us. As it transforms us, we see more and more clearly quite how living and active the word of God really is.

> **In short**
> The Bible is a living active text that transforms us and reveals to us not only more about who God is but more about who we are.

For discussion

- Have you ever had the experience of feeling that something—whether it be a piece of writing, a film, a song, work of art, or in fact anything else—has told you something about yourself? Discuss some of these experiences together.

- How might we read the Bible differently if we took the Bible seriously as living and active?

- What kind of qualities might we need to bring to our reading of the Bible if we want to be open to the Bible "reading us" and telling us more about ourselves?

The thoughts and intentions of our hearts

In verse 12 the author of Hebrews goes on to use what is, to our ear, a somewhat surprising metaphor—the word of God is a two-edged sword. What this refers to is its sharpness. In the ancient world there was little as sharp as a sword. Perhaps a more resonant image for us today might be a precision-sharpened kitchen knife. Both swords and knives are able to get between two things that seem to be joined seamlessly together, and to pry and slice them apart.

The point of the image appears at the end of verse 12. The word of God is able to judge the thoughts and intentions of the heart. It is worth noting that in Hebrew thinking the heart was associated with thinking as well as feeling, and Old Testament writers located thought processes, decisions, and intentions in the heart. In other words, much of what we would associate with the head, they associated with the heart.

The problem with our thoughts and intentions, whether we locate them in the head or the heart, is that it can sometimes be impossible for us to determine why we did something. Was it for a good motive or a bad one? Were we caring more for others or for ourselves?

Were we caring more for others or for ourselves?

Could the decision we made be described as holy or not? Sometimes the reasons for our decisions and actions are as much a mystery to us as they are to others. But the word of God can help us here.

Hebrews 4:12 refers to the word of God as a tool for discernment. In situations where we simply cannot tell "joints from marrow," good intention from bad, what is life-giving or life-denying, the sharp edge of the word of God living and active can help. This is not a straightforward process. The Bible is not like a fortune cookie that we crack open to provide an immediate answer. Instead it shapes us and forms us. Over days, weeks, months, and years of reading the Bible, we can learn to sift and weigh our intentions and those of others, to begin to recognize what fits in the realm of God's vision for the world—a vision governed by righteousness, justice, and love—and what does not.

Jesus, the Word of God, sees everyone and everything for who and what they truly are. As Hebrews observes, God's gaze is one of compassion that sympathizes with our weaknesses, but it is also clear and true. As we learn more from the word of God we can adopt that gaze as our own and begin to see ourselves as Jesus, the Word of God, sees us.

> **In short**
> The word of God can help us to discern more clearly what God's vision is for the world and whether our thoughts and intentions fit properly within that vision.

For discussion

- From your reading of the Bible so far, what do you think God's vision for the world is?

- What might you need to do to enable this vision to impact the things that you think, say, and do?

- If you were to approach the Bible as a "two-edged sword" that is able to "judge the thoughts and intentions of the heart," how might you need to read it so that it can help you discern the truth?

Journeying On

Here are some verses from the Bible to reflect on this week, one for each of six days:

Steadfast love and faithfulness will meet; righteousness and peace will kiss each other (Psalm 85:10).

Happy are those who observe justice, who do righteousness at all times (Psalm 106:3).

He has told you, O mortal, what is good; and what does the LORD require of you but to do justice, and to love kindness, and to walk humbly with your God? (Micah 6:8).

Grace, mercy, and peace will be with us from God the Father and from Jesus Christ, the Father's Son, in truth and love (2 John 1:3).

My soul thirsts for God, for the living God. When shall I come and behold the face of God? (Psalm 42:2).

Bear one another's burdens, and in this way you will fulfill the law of Christ (Galatians 6:2).

Concluding Prayers

God of all wisdom,
send your spirit upon us
so that our hearts might burn within us
as we read your word
and in reading discover who we are
and who you yearn that we might become.
Amen.

As our Savior taught us, so we pray,
Our Father... (see pp. 5-6)

Wisdom for the Journey

Our greatest protection in this life is self-knowledge so that we do not become enslaved to delusion, and end up trying to defend a person who does not exist.

GREGORY OF NYSSA (C. 330-94)

Holy Scripture confronts the eye of our mind like a mirror in order that we may see our inward face in it. It is there that we come to know both our ugliness and our beauty. In it we can tell what progress we are making and how far we actually are from real improvement.

GREGORY THE GREAT (540-604)

The Scriptures we are commanded to search. They are commended that search and study them. They are reproved that were unskilllful in them, or slow to believe them. They can make us wise unto salvation. If we be ignorant, they will instruct us; if out of the way, they will bring us home; if out of order, they will reform us; if in heaviness, comfort us; if dull, quicken us; if cold, inflame us.

PREFACE TO THE FIRST EDITION OF THE AUTHORIZED VERSION OF THE BIBLE, 1611

SESSION SIX:
DAILY BREAD

pilgrim

In this session we think a little more about making Bible reading a part of our regular life and prayer.

Opening Prayers

I will extol you, my God and King, and bless your name for ever and ever.
Every day we will bless you.

Every day I will bless you, and praise your name for ever and ever.
Every day we will bless you.

Great is the LORD, and greatly to be praised; his greatness is unsearchable.
Every day we will bless you.

One generation shall laud your works to another, and shall declare your mighty acts.
Every day we will bless you.

On the glorious splendor of your majesty, and on your wondrous works, I will meditate.
Every day we will bless you.

The might of your awesome deeds shall be proclaimed, and I will declare your greatness.
Every day we will bless you.

They shall celebrate the fame of your abundant goodness, and shall sing aloud of your righteousness.
Every day we will bless you.

The LORD is gracious and merciful, slow to anger and abounding in steadfast love.
Every day we will bless you.

PSALM 145:1-8

Blessed Lord, who caused all holy Scriptures to be written for our learning: help us so to hear them, to read, mark, learn, and inwardly digest them that, through patience, and the comfort of your holy word, we may embrace and for ever hold fast the hope of everlasting life, which you have given us in our Savior Jesus Christ, who is alive and reigns with you, in the unity of the Holy Spirit, one God, now and for ever. **Amen.**

Conversation

Share with the group any reflections you have had on the Bible verses from the Journeying On section last week.

Bread has long been the staple diet in some cultures, and in others it has been something else, like rice. What is your equivalent to "daily bread"?

Reflecting on Scripture

Reading

"Everyone then who hears these words of mine and acts on them will be like a wise man who built his house on rock. 25The rain fell, the floods came, and the winds blew and beat on that house, but it did not fall, because it had been founded on rock. 26And everyone who hears these words of mine and does not act on them will be like a foolish man who built his house on sand. 27The rain fell, and the floods came, and the winds blew and beat against that house, and it fell—and great was its fall!" 28Now when Jesus had finished saying these things, the crowds were astounded at his teaching, 29for he taught them as one having authority, and not as their scribes.

MATTHEW 7:24-29

Explanatory note

This passage is the final part of the great collection of the teaching of Jesus in Matthew 5–7 known as the Sermon on the Mount. The teaching is addressed to the disciples of Jesus (5:1). This final passage underlines the importance of not simply listening to Jesus' teaching but putting it into practice.

"The scribes" is one of the names used in Matthew for the Jewish teachers of the law. Their way of teaching was normally to quote other authorities—"Rabbi Hillel says such and such"—rather than to speak in the first person.

● Read the passage through once.
● Keep a few moments' silence.

- Read the passage a second time with different voices.
- Invite everyone to say aloud a word or phrase that strikes them.
- Read the passage a third time.
- Share together what this word or phrase might mean and what questions it raises.

Reflection   STEVEN CROFT

The story of the temptation of Jesus is told in Matthew's Gospel and in Luke. Jesus responds to the temptation to command stones to become bread with these words from Deuteronomy: "One does not live by bread alone, but by every word that comes from the mouth of God" (Matthew 4:4, and see also Luke 4:4).

> God's word gives us food for the spirit.

The word of God, the Scriptures, are like bread: as bread gives us physical nourishment, so God's word gives us food for the spirit, to sustain us in our discipleship and on our journey.

Put that thought together with the line of the Lord's Prayer that says: "Give us this day our daily bread" and then ask yourself the question: How often should we read and reflect on the Scriptures?

For most Christians, coming to God's living word, Jesus, through God's written word, the Bible, is a regular, daily discipline. We live in a time and place when we can have access to a printed Bible in our own homes and where most—but not all—adults can read. In earlier generations people would have had to rely on learning passages of Scripture by heart and reflecting on them each day. But the pattern from earliest times has been for disciples to have a pattern or rule of life that includes daily prayer. At the center of the prayer is thoughtful reflection on the Scriptures: listening to God.

Good habits take time to build up. You will need to experiment and find a pattern for prayer and Bible reading that works for you. For most people it helps to have a regular time and place—a special chair or corner of a room—and to have ready access to your own copy of the Bible.

Many people also find it helpful to have a set pattern of prayers that are themselves based on Scripture. One term for this pattern of prayer is a "Daily Office." "Office" in this sense means not a room with a desk and a computer but an offering of our prayer and praise to God. Morning (or Evening) Prayer for Episcopalians is a way of praying the Scriptures through reading the psalms each day and a short passage from the Old and the New Testaments. This kind of pattern offers a regular, balanced diet from the Scriptures.

> **In short**
>
> It is good to read and reflect on the Bible regularly, in a balanced way, and to do this in the context of daily prayer.

For discussion

- What is your present pattern of prayer and Bible reading? How do you find it helpful and sustaining?

- Do you use any particular prayer books, apps, or Bible-reading notes to support your reading of Scripture?

How to read the Bible

Whenever you read the Bible or hear it read as the Church gathers together, pray that God will speak to you and to the whole community through the Scriptures. The prayer that Eli taught Samuel is a good one to learn by heart and to use regularly: "Speak, LORD, for your servant is listening" (1 Samuel 3:9).

Listening is rarely easy. According to 1 Kings 19:12, God speaks gently and softly. His word came to Elijah the prophet not through an earthquake, wind, or fire but through the sound of sheer silence. In Psalm 46 we are told: "Be still, and know that I am God!"

This means taking time with a text to read it carefully and normally several times (as we have done throughout *Pilgrim*). It may mean looking up any difficult or unfamiliar words. It will mean pondering carefully

> Listening is
> rarely easy.

words and phrases that strike us, discerning in each passage and each verse what fresh insight God has for us today. It may mean learning short phrases or verses by heart so we can return to them again and again as we have need.

What we draw from the Scriptures will vary day by day and year by year. Often we may be drawn deeper into an encounter with God. Sometimes we will receive new insight into ourselves or our own lives. There will be moments of deep encouragement and occasionally challenge. Our minds may be changed. Sometimes there will be questions that we need to take to a friend who can help us.

Finally, to listen in the Bible always carries the meaning of to obey, to be like the second house builder, the one who listens to the words of Jesus and goes away and puts them into practice. Attending to the Scriptures, day by day, means allowing them to shape our words, our actions, and our lives.

In short

Listening to God through the Scriptures is demanding, dynamic, and life-giving.

For discussion

- What would be your top three things to aim at in your reading of the Bible in the coming year?
- How will you continue to reflect with others on your habits of prayer and Bible reading and the way they feed your Christian life?

Journeying On

Here are some verses for you to reflect on this week, one each day for six days:

Upon you I have leaned from my birth; it was you who took me from my mother's womb. My praise is continually of you (Psalm 71:6).

The law of the LORD is perfect, reviving the soul; the decrees of the LORD are sure, making wise the simple; the precepts of the LORD are right, rejoicing the heart; the commandment of the LORD is clear, enlightening the eyes; the fear of the LORD is pure, enduring for ever; the ordinances of the LORD are true and righteous altogether (Psalm 19:7-9).

For a day in your courts is better than a thousand elsewhere. I would rather be a doorkeeper in the house of my God than live in the tents of wickedness (Psalm 84:10).

Rejoice always, pray without ceasing, give thanks in all circumstances; for this is the will of God in Christ Jesus for you (1 Thessalonians 5: 16-18).

The grace of the Lord Jesus Christ, the love of God, and the communion of the Holy Spirit be with all of you (2 Corinthians 13:13).

For I am convinced that neither death, nor life, nor angels, nor rulers, nor things present, nor things to come, nor powers, nor height, nor depth, nor anything else in all creation, will be able to separate us from the love of God in Christ Jesus our Lord (Romans 8:38-39).

Concluding Prayers

Living Word
Give us grace to be still and silent,
To quieten our fears
To listen to your word
That you may quicken our spirits
And guide our lives
Through the grace of the Holy Spirit
And to the glory of God the Father
Amen.

As our Savior taught us, so we pray,
Our Father... (see pp. 5-6)

Wisdom for the Journey

When God created human beings he made them "in his own image and likeness." He does not imprint this image exteriorly on us, but within us. It could not be seen in you as long as your house was dirty, full of junk and rubbish. But once you let the Word of God clear the great pile of earth that is weighing down your soul, then the image of the heavenly king will again shine out in you. The maker of this image is the Son of God. And he is a craftsman of such surpassing skill that though his image may indeed become obscured by our neglect, it can never be destroyed by evil. The image of God always remains within you.

ORIGEN (*C.* 185–*C.* 254)

An old monk said, "The prophets wrote books, then our Fathers put their teaching into practice. Those who came after then learnt the Scriptures by heart. Then came this present generation who have copied them out, and then put them into their window seats without using them."

ANON (4TH CENTURY)

When you study God's word be thankful for what you have received, and do not be saddened that an abundance still remains. What you have received and attained is your present share, while what is left will be your heritage.

EPHREM OF SYRIA (C. 306–373)

Beginning to read the Bible seriously is rather like visiting a vast art museum. We are bewildered at first by the profusion of images and tend to survey them all in a daze, pausing before only a few of the most famous or striking works. But if we begin to make regular visits we learn to contemplate just one object at a time and let it work on our imagination. In time a single painting or sculpture can show us many things about life. In the same way one scriptural symbol can in time work changes in us through the power of the Spirit.

MARTIN L. SMITH (1947–)

Notes

Opening and Concluding Prayers

Common Worship: Services and Prayers for the Church of England, London, Church House Publishing, 2000.

Opening Prayers for Session One (p. 384), Session Two (p. 382), Session Three (p. 384), Session Four (p. 47), Session Six (p. 390) and Concluding Prayer for Session Six (p. 422).

Session One

Ephrem of Syria (*c.* 306–73), *Commentary on the Diatessaron*, 1, 18.
John Cassian (*c.* 360–435), *Conferences*, 14, 10.
Isidore of Seville (*c.* 560–636), *The Book of Maxims*, 3, 8.
Guigo V (1083–1136), Prior of la Grande Chartreuse, *Letter to the Brethren of the Mount of God*, 8. 31.
Martin L. Smith (1947–), *The Word is Very Near You*, London, Darton, Longman & Todd, 1990, p. 55.

Session Two

Ambrose of Milan (*c.* 334–97), *Commentary on the Psalm 1*, 9.
Jerome (*c.* 342–420), Letter to a young priest, written in 394.
Isidore of Seville (*c.* 560–636), *The Book of Maxims*, 3, 8.
William Tyndale (1494–1536), Epistle to the Reader, in his translation of the New Testament, 1526.

Session Three

Origen (*c.* 185–*c.* 254), *Homily 1 "On Genesis,"* 4.
Columbanus (*c.* 543–615), *Instruction 13 on "Christ the Fount of Life."*
Bernard of Clairvaux (1090–1153), *Sermon 5 "On Advent,"* 2.

Session Four

Ephrem of Syria (*c.* 306–73), *Commentary on the Diatessaron*, 1, 18.
John Cassian (*c.* 360–435), *Conferences*, 10, 11.
Benedict of Nursia (480–550), *Rule*, Prologue.
Isaac of Nineveh (seventh century), *The Ascetical Treatises*, 73.
William Ewart Gladstone, Prime Minister, advice to his eldest son, from *Correspondence on Church and Religion*, ed. D. C. Lathbury, London, 1910.
John Macmurray (1891–1976), *Reason and Emotion*, London, 1935, p. 46.

Session Five

Gregory of Nyssa (*c.* 330–94), *Homily 2 "On the Song of Songs."*
Gregory the Great (540–604), *Commentary on the Book of Job*.
From the Preface to the first edition of the Authorized Version of the Bible, 1611.

Session Six

Origen (*c.* 185–*c.* 254), *Homily 1 "On Genesis."* 4.
Anon (fourth century), *Sayings of the Desert Fathers and Mothers*.
Ephrem of Syria (*c.* 306–73), *Commentary on the Diatessaron*, 1, 18.
Martin L. Smith, *The Word is Very Near You*, London: Darton, Longman & Todd, 1990, p. 64.